THE CHURCH IN
THE NEW
SOCIAL ORDER

THE CHURCH IN THE NEW SOCIAL ORDER

EMIL BRUNNER

An address delivered to the
National Congress of the Free Church
Federal Council, Cardiff,
on 26th March, 1952

SCM PRESS LTD
56 BLOOMSBURY STREET
LONDON

First published 1952

*Printed in Great Britain by Tonbridge Printers Ltd.,
Peach Hall Works, Tonbridge, Kent*

THE CHURCH IN
THE NEW SOCIAL ORDER

I HAVE to begin with a most serious apology. The topic I am going to speak about is not, as indicated on your programme, 'The Freedom of the Church in the Modern State' but 'The Church in the New Social Order'. This was the topic which was first indicated to me when I was asked to come to this Assembly and give a lecture. It was only later that this topic was changed into the one of the freedom of the Church. Somehow this change did not take hold of me. It was only after I had done the whole work of preparation that I received the printed programme and then became aware of my mistake. But then the time was too short for me to start again and prepare another paper.

Now, after this apology, I must add a confession, namely, that I am really glad that I had worked on the first and not on the second topic, because I find it a lot more interesting. The freedom of the Church may have been a real problem for Germany under Hitler, and is of course a real problem for the Russian Church under the Communist dictators. But it can hardly be called an urgent problem for you British Christians, and, therefore, to speak about it would have placed you in the position of spectators. It would not have been for you—to use a modern expression—an existential, but a more or less academic problem.

Well, whether you agree with me in this estimate or not, you have to put up with my choice, and I can only hope that you will find, after all, my error pardonable and not too disadvantageous for this Assembly.

The topic then is, 'The Church in the New Social Order'. Even for this topic I have to make a brief remark as a preface. By the new social order, I suppose, you understand the present order of Great Britain, that is, the changes which have taken place in the structure of your society—particularly since the end of World War II. Now, being a Continental European and not a Britisher, I do not know this new social order in your country as you know it, that is, by personal daily experience. On the other hand, the outsider, seeing certain things from a distance, may see them more objectively. Let me say from the start that by this new social order the United Kingdom presents a kind of geographical paradox. Britain is no more, as it used to be, half-way between western Europe and America, but it is now half-way between western Europe and the East. Some of you may have heard the address I gave three years ago on the theme, The Church between East and West, and perhaps remember my sharp distinction of the two civilisations. But now the question is: What is the situation of the Church in this new social order which places your country, paradoxically enough, *between* Europe and the East? I am not asked whether this new social order is a good thing or not; I am asked: What is the place and what are the specific problems which face the Church in this new social order which we have to take as given?

Our first question has to be: Does *any* given social order affect and interest the Church at all? This is not a merely academic question. It is not, amongst representatives of the Christian Church, necessary to state that the interest of the Church for the social order can only be an indirect one. It is not the primary, not the essential task of the Church to create, to change, to improve the social order. The task of the Church lies beyond any social order, because its task is to preach the Gospel of Jesus Christ, the Kingdom of God which transcends all social orders, the good and bad alike. The immediate, primary task of the Church is not to preach and to fight for a social programme, but to preach the message of redemption and eternal life.

Since the time when Karl Marx, more than anyone

else, directed the interest of Western mankind towards the social order, a remarkable change has taken place, within the Church as well as outside it. The dictum of Marx that religion is opium of the people, meaning that it takes away the vital attention of men from the task of making the social order just and human, and directs it towards a fantastic, transcendent aim beyond reality, is a negative evaluation of the message and work of the Church which has not failed to impress the Churches as well as those outside. It made Christians eager to disprove Marx's word by adopting, in large measure, his view that to change the social order from an unjust one into a just one was the real task of man, whether Christian or secularist. This shift, from the previous false disinterestedness with regard to the social order, to a passionate co-operation with the forces which made this betterment, or revolution of the social order, their main and only purpose, has been both wholesome and dangerous, not to say detrimental. It has been wholesome, in so far as the Church had, indeed, bitterly failed in its responsibility for the structure of the society in which men, women and children have to live; it had failed to create social conditions worthy of a Christian society and wholesome to live in, spiritually and physically. It has been detrimental, in so far as a good many church people were seduced into believing that, in fact, the change of the social order was the real, supreme task of everybody, including the Church.

This shift of emphasis within the Church could not take place, however, without a major change in the interpretation of the Gospel. This change in the understanding of the New Testament Gospels is concerned primarily with the biblical conception of the Kingdom of God. The Kingdom of God, which is the unmistakable centre of the New Testament Gospel, was now understood to be more or less identical with the social order which man is called upon to transform from an unjust one into a just one; from an inhuman one into a human one. It was by this substitution that it became possible to make the interest in a new social order the supreme purpose of Christianity, and thereby to evade the judgement of Marx's dictum that religion is opium of the people. But, of course, this substitution was a tremendous falsification. The Kingdom of God which the New Testament preaches is not a new social order which man can and must create. The Kingdom of God is not at all something which man can create. It is the new life, the new condition of mankind and of the world at large, which God alone can bring about; something which comes from beyond man's own doing and striving.

That does not mean, however, that this New Testament conception of the Kingdom has no relation to man's responsibility for the social order. On the contrary, the more man is filled with hope for the Kingdom of God the more he feels responsible and becomes active in bringing about a just and human social order. The belief in eternal life and the hope of the Kingdom, if they are right, are the very opposite of Marx's opium; they are the motors and the driving power behind man's efforts to bring in a new social order. It may be said with fairness that it was particularly that aspect of the Reformation movement which took its origin in Zurich and Geneva which gave a splendid proof of the necessary connection between the hope in the eternal Kingdom of God and the vigour of the ethical forces directed towards the establishment of a better social order. Still, the first thing to know is that the Kingdom of God and any man-created social order, however good, just and human it may be, are two different things, separate from each other like heaven and earth, like eternity and time, like grace and work, like God's own doing and man's doing.

As this point is of prime importance, let me dwell upon it a little longer. The Kingdom of God cannot be identified with any *order*. Even when we think of the Kingdom of God as something not merely in the future, but also in present experience, as indeed we should, the Kingdom of God is entirely different from any *order*. The *Ekklesia* of the New Testament, which is to be understood as the present and experienced form of the Kingdom of God, is not an order. The *Ekklesia* of the New Testament is something entirely personal, namely, the communion between Christ and His people, who are His by faith, and the communion of these people with one another through their communion in Christ. The essence of the Kingdom is love; God's love given to man, man's love towards man. Love, however, cannot be institutionalised. The *Ekklesia* is in no way an institution, an order, but a personal life flowing from beyond the temporal world; it is God's own life sharing itself with men through the Mediator, Christ. The *Ekklesia* is something exclusively personal, consisting of the Person of Christ and the persons of the believers who, by faith, are in Christ. And by this token the *Ekklesia* cannot be an order, whether a social order or a church order. An order, however good and just, is something impersonal, abstract. An order belongs always to the world, and not to the Kingdom of God. It might be, at its best, a reflection of the Kingdom of God, a shadow, a by-product of the Kingdom, but even then it is of the world, or, to use a biblical conception, it is flesh, not spirit.

Therefore, whilst it is true that the Church has the task to strive and work for a just and human social order, this can never be her primary, her essential task; it cannot be in the centre, but merely on the periphery.

This does not mean that this task is of little importance, but it does mean that it is never the *main* task of the Church. The Church has to preach the Gospel of the Kingdom, of life eternal, of eternal salvation; and she has to live in it. I hope you will not misunderstand this as a return to a pietistic, individualistic conception of the Gospel. The New Testament idea and reality of the *Ekklesia* is not only the most personal, it is also the most social or, better, the most communal thing. It is more social than any Socialism, it is more communal than any Communism. Socialism or Communism, even in their highest possible form, are orders, and, for that reason, they are of this world.

The first thing, then, to be said about the Church's task in the new social order, is that it is the same as in any other previous or future social order. It has to proclaim the Kingdom of God which transcends all social orders, those of the future no less than those of the past, the socialist order no less than the capitalist.

The new socialist order, then, about which you ask, has not changed in any fundamental or essential way the situation or the task of the Church; whether the Church has to live in a social order like that of the Roman Empire, or in the feudal order of the Middle Ages, or in the bourgeois capitalist order of the post-Reformation era, or in the socialist or semi-socialist order, which is yours—the task of the Church is essentially the same. The Gospel we have to preach is the same as that of St. Augustine, of St. Francis, of Luther, Calvin or William Booth, or Johann Christoph Blumhardt.

But, whilst this is the first, it is by no means the only thing to be said about the question: The Church in the new social order. I am not so unrealistic as not to acknowledge that every social order presents a specific challenge to the Church, and that it creates for it specific problems. Let us now face them, after having plainly stated that no social order, however good, is of the nature of the Kingdom of God, and that no social order, however bad, makes the task of the Church impossible. Still, the Church in Great Britain can look back upon something which many Christians have been striving for during two or three generations, and which is now achieved. In this country it was not so much Karl Marx, but men like Carlyle, Kingsley and Maurice, who were able to arouse the social conscience of the people, and of Christians in particular, who strove to make them see the appalling conditions of the industrial workers and their families, and who *did* stir a new sense and desire for a new social order, more just and more *humane*. I shall never forget the enthusiastic hope and the prophetic call for justice which flamed in my great teacher Leonhard Raganz, the founder of the continental religious socialist movement, who made us look up with reverence to those men in Great Britain who were leading the fight for a better social order, men like Keir Hardie, Philip Snowden, Ramsey Macdonald, Will Crooks and other Labour leaders, fighting for socialism against capitalism in the name of Jesus Christ. It was in London, in the autumn of 1913, that I began to translate the speeches of these men which had been delivered during 'the Labour week' at Browning settlement, in order to make them known in German. Then, later, came the time when I worked together, hand in hand, so to speak, with that great fighter for a just social order, William Temple, before and during the Oxford conference of 1937, after I had written my book on ethics, *The Divine Imperative*. All of us felt it to be the task of the Church to work for that new social order which has now become a reality in your country.

Now, this aim being achieved, what do we think about it and what is our next task? It is certainly neither easy nor necessary to analyse our feelings with regard to this new social order. I want to point to one feature only—we all feel that the task for the future is very different from that of the past. Whether you are satisfied or disappointed with this new social order, one thing is clear; the task of the Church does not lie any more—if it ever did—in the sphere of the structural change of society. One can say, the Church now has her hands free again for her real, immediate task, namely, leading men and women to Jesus Christ. Whilst this may be felt to be a net gain, one has to be aware of a loss connected with it. In the time when church people were fighting for a new order, an order of justice, they were looked upon by the working people as comrades striving for the same aims as they themselves were striving for. Now this link does not exist any more, and this may be one of the reasons for the fact that the Church has lost much of its previous popularity.

But, apart from this, does the new social order make the task of the Church easier or more difficult? My answer would be—both easier and more difficult. The new social order has certainly done a great deal to remove inequality and to improve the lot of the working population. The so-called middle-class and the so-called working-class have been strongly approximated to each other, and by that the resentment of the latter against the former has more or less lost its basis. The Church to a large degree benefits from this disappearance of social resentment. One would expect it to be easier to bring the Gospel to people whose outward condition somehow measures up to the demands of justice and humanity, and who feel themselves equal with the rest of the nation.

On the other hand, and this is to show why the task

of the Church has become more difficult, we should not be blind to the fact that in all measures of socialisation or collectivisation there is, unavoidably, a tendency to depersonalisation. The centre of personality is responsibility. Every step towards a collectivist society inevitably tends towards a decrease of the sense of responsibility, towards shifting responsibility from the individual person towards the collectivity, the State. Furthermore, where the State more and more gets into its hands the fate, the well-being or evil-being of all the people, it is looked upon more and more as the earthly God. Man does not need a Saviour God any more, because, by means of the State, he can work out salvation for himself. This is true of technical civilisation as such. Where men live more in man-made surroundings than in God's creation they are apt to forget their dependence on God, the Creator. Where men have become accustomed to expect from the State every kind of relief, every measure of betterment, they begin to think that man is capable of being his own saviour by means of the improvement of the State.

This is true, of course, in a much higher degree of the perfectly totalitarian State than it is of your half-way socialist State. But let me, as a Continental, insert here a few words about your new British social order.

Whatever one thinks about it, one thing cannot be denied: it is something typically and exclusively British.

I mean this as something essentially positive. Such a socialisation as yours would have had, in any other country but yours, results which in your country were avoided only because of the unique strength of your liberal tradition which, on the whole, is Christian. To give one single example. All British universities are receiving large subsidies from the State, and still have been able to keep their autonomy intact. This is, for us Continentals, something like a miracle, because with us it always goes according to the saying—'Who pays the piper calls the tune'. Not so with you, because there is still at work that most beneficent factor—the liberal Christian tradition. However, I know from a good many university men, even those who stand for the new social order, that they are afraid that in the course of some years this wonderful autonomy of your highest schools of learning will fall a victim to the State.

I said at the beginning, England is half-way between western Europe and the East. This would be much more evident if you were not living on an old Christian liberal inheritance which prevents collectivism from appearing in its more dangerous features. In the same measure, however, as this Christian element becomes weaker, the more inhuman and depersonalised features of the collectivist structure of society must appear more markedly.

But whatever your estimate of the achievements of the new social order may be, on one point most of you would certainly agree: you should not seek the solution of the unsolved problems of your nation in further structural changes in the line of further socialisation. If you should do this, all the same, you would necessarily end in the totalitarian State which, I think, all of us recognize as something utterly undesirable. What a completely socialised or collectivised society means we can now see clearly in the east of Europe. The history of our own generation has taught us that complete socialisation is identical with the totalitarian State. However, according to a remark of the great Swiss historian, Jakob Burckhardt, 'History teaches that History teaches nothing'. He meant that people will not learn from history. And, indeed, there are still people who believe that you can have complete socialisation and still keep your liberal democracy. I should call them fools who have not learned the lesson of history.

Of course, nobody doubts that the new social order which you have created is not paradise. Everybody agrees on that. However, at this point it should be the Church which unambiguously should raise her voice to say, *No* social order can be paradise. A social order, however just and human, can be at best only a frame into which a truly human life can be poured.

It is a fantastic Utopian illusion to believe that by

making the framework—the structure of society, what we call the social order—more social, that is, more socialised or collectivised, you make the life of men more human. It is exactly the task or office of the Church to oppose this Utopian illusion, and to distinguish between social order as the frame of life and life itself, truly personal and, at the same time, truly communist.

If we take an optimistic view of the new social order, as most of us probably do, we may say, It has created a fair balance between the interests of the individual and those of the collectivity. To go further in the direction of socialisation would lead towards a disturbance of this balance in favour of collectivity.

What then can the necessary improvement be? Let me put it in two corresponding concepts, personalisation and communalisation within the given framework of this new social order. This is not the Church's own task, of which I am going to speak presently, but it is closer to it than anything relating to the social order, as such. As an example of what I mean by these two words let us take the relation between employer and employee within the given framework of the new social order. There could be and should be a closer co-operation between the two main factors, the employers and the employees on a basis of mutual respect and recognition of the necessary function of the partner on the other side. The Marxist theory of class struggle is superseded; it can and it must be replaced by co-operation, by the insight that both sides have a common interest, that they are partners in a common enterprise. Hand in hand must go a new evaluation of work as a vocation. It is the great merit of Dr. J. H. Oldham that for a couple of years he has been stressing this point as the next great task of ecumenical studies with regard to the social problem, and that he gave an excellent lead by writing a little book which deserves to become a classic on the Christian understanding of work, under the title *Work in Modern Society*. Personalisation and communalisation of human relationships is *the* great social task of the present and next generation.

Still, as I have just said, this is not yet the Church's own and exclusive task. What *is* it? We are in the habit of saying; The Church's primary and essential task is to preach the Word of God. And this is correct. Only, I would add, in our age this task also acquires its specific form, both theologically and practically. If it has become the supreme task of society to personalise and to communalise the relations of men in the new social order, it is the specific task of the Churches of this day to personalise and to communalise the preaching of the Word of God. Preaching in the traditional sense of the word, whether in the Sunday service of the congregation of believers, or in evangelism, that is, preaching to those outside the Church, seems to lack more and more the unique importance it used to have in previous times. Am I wrong, however, if I say: Both the Church and theology are about to discover a double fact: the sociological meaning of the Word and the theological meaning of community; or, to put it in one concept, the unity of the Word and Sacrament. I shall now try to develop this a little further.

The Word of God is not the same as a doctrine, something which can be grasped by theological concepts; the Word of God is the creation of communion, communion between God and man, communion also between man and man. Faith, that faith which the preaching of the Word of God is intended to create— what is it? Is it not this, that God breaks through that wall of isolation which stands between God and man, as well as between man and man? Faith in God through Christ—is it not this, that man ceases to be an individual centred round his self-interest? Faith, then, what is it if not communion with God and communion with man? Faith, is it not what in modern terminology we might call communal existence, and is it not what the New Testament calls *Ekklesia?*

Now let us consider what in the New Testament the so-called Sacraments mean. If a pagan was baptised was it not this, that he received the Holy Spirit and was, so to speak, grafted into the Body of Christ? If

[21]

the disciples ate bread and drank the cup of wine in memory of the death of their Lord, was it not that they experienced the presence of their Lord Jesus, and by that were formed into His Body? Sacramental existence is the same thing as communal existence through communion with the Christ who is the Spirit. Word and Sacrament not only *belong* together—that is what we all learnt in our catechism; Word and Sacrament *are* one and the same thing, namely, God's action by which He makes men one with Him and one with one another, through the gift of His Son and of His Spirit.

Seen from this angle, our traditional church service as well as our traditional doctrines and theologies appear to be individualistic on the one hand, intellectualist and collectivist on the other. One goes to church to get the Word of God individually; one goes to the service of the Holy Supper in order to receive the Sacramental gift individually. But this individualistic approach is not adequate to the meaning either of the Word or of the Sacrament. Our theologies have always emphasised the transforming character of the Word and of the Sacrament; but they failed to emphasise that this transformation is essentially the transformation of an individual into a member of the Body of Christ. Our Reformers, Luther, Zwingli and Calvin, were right in denying that the Sacrament is the transformation of the elements, bread and wine, into the Body of Christ. But they did not see as clearly that indeed the Sacrament *is* a transformation, not of the elements, but of the persons who eat and drink, into the Body of Christ. The Roman doctrine was right when it said: In the Holy Communion the Body of Christ is produced; but it was terribly wrong when it said that this Body of Christ is the transubstantiated bread and wine. The Body of Christ which the Sacrament produces is no other than that which in the whole of the New Testament is meant by 'the Body of Christ' as the communion of those whom Christ unites with God, with Himself and with one another.

And what then, in the New Testament, is the *Ekklesia?* We usually translate this Greek word by our modern words Church or *Kirche* or *Eglise*. This is not wrong in itself, but it becomes entirely wrong if by Church or *Kirche* we mean—as we mostly do—an institution. The New Testament *Ekklesia* is never an institution; it is always and exclusively a communion of persons, namely the communion of God through Christ with the believers, and the communion of the believers or disciples through Christ with one another. But never have any of the apostles thought of *Ekklesia* in terms of an institution, an impersonal collectivity. Correlative to the individualistic conception of the work of the

Word of God in the individual is the collectivist, institutionalist conception of the Church.

In the New Testament, however, the three concepts, Word of God, Sacrament, Church, form a unity by their essential relatedness to communion. Christ forms His Body by the Word and by the Sacraments, and this Body is the *Ekklesia*. Now, so far we have pointed to the rediscovery of New Testament realities in theology.

But at the same time, when this theological rediscovery was made, church practice has begun to move on parallel lines. In different parts of the Christian world Churches have discovered anew the basic importance of the group and cell principle, be it as a principle of evangelisation or of—if I may use this word—Christian nurture. In other parts there has been discovered the importance of professional units as nuclei of church life. Again, in different places, Christian people have rediscovered the function of communal work in the formation of Christian communal life. In one word, in many ways and many forms the Church of Christ is about to rediscover the essential importance of group formation, of communal existence, for the process of becoming a Christian and of growing to spiritual maturity. Many of us have experienced how much more real the Lord's Supper becomes if it is not isolated from ordinary working life, but if it is taken by a group of people who are engaged in some common effort, and who by this have become a live social unit, not only working, but eating, sleeping, playing, singing and praying together.

I hope that by now the two abstract words which I used a minute ago have got more content: the discovery of the sociological meaning of the Word of God and the theological meaning of community. Let me try to combine the two into one: the rediscovery of sacramental existence.

It may not be useless at this point to throw a glance outside, into the world beyond the precincts of the Church, into the general spiritual or ideological movements of our time. In the chaos of spiritual efforts and tendencies of all sorts, two main movements are more or less clearly distinguishable as characteristic of our age: Communism on the one hand, existentialism on the other. Now these two are, of course, of a very different nature, in some ways they may be called opposites. But alongside this obvious dissimilarity there is also noticeable an important similarity. Both of them are trying to give a new interpretation to truth and to community by relating them to one another. The Communist, as you know, does not recognise objective truth. Truth to him is the Communist system and ideology outside of which there is only lies. To get at truth you have to become a believing Communist, and, if you are, you do not bother any more about what the outsiders call truth.

The existentialist, on the other hand, does not believe in objective truth, because to him truth is something to be related to existence in its totality, not something intellectually abstract. Real truth can be grasped only by those who let themselves be engaged in their lived totality. Truth is not an objective 'it', but truth is 'being with'.

Now, most of us, again and again, feel repelled by Communism as well as by existentialism. We see their failures, their absurdities and impossibilities. We should not see these negative characters only. We should distinguish between the deeper longing and intuition, and the obvious failure of both to fulfil this longing. The Communist seeks (as the very word indicates which is the sign of the deepest motive) community. He is, as everybody knows, anti-individualistic. But instead of finding and creating community he is finding and creating a mere substitute for community, namely, collectivity. Instead of opposing community to individualism he merely opposes collectivity instead. And collectivity, in its turn, is a product of atomisation, of the utmost isolation of individuals. Communism forms society, like briquettes of pulverised individuals, by outward pressure. A briquette looks like something compact, something whole; as a matter of fact it is compressed dust particles; it is nothing like an organic unity. It is a mechanism, not a community.

On the other hand, the existentialist does not find what he is after, namely, existential truth. His efforts to find it end in despair and nausea. It is not by chance that the first book of fiction by Sartre, the best-known French existentialist, was entitled *Nausea*. The existentialist effort ends in a kind of nihilism and an arbitrary, groundless, meaningless freedom. Even Heidegger's great philosophical venture has ended in an æsthetic brand of nihilism.

Why is this so? Because both Communism and existentialism are atheistic. Both of them have accepted the negation of God of the bourgeois society of the nineteenth century, to which otherwise they were so radically opposed. Both Communism and existentialism have sensed the problem, you might even say they have put it, but they cannot solve it. Their answer is no answer because they do not know that truth which, at the same time, is community and existential.

And this truth is God revealed in Jesus Christ. You may call the Gospel existential truth, because it cannot be grasped objectively but only in an act of total personal surrender; you may call it community-truth, because it cannot be had outside of the community with Christ and His people.

So we have come back to the point from which we

started this excursion into the world of our age. It seems to be the task of us Christians of this age to rediscover the unity of truth and community, of truth and existence, in the sacramental existence in Jesus Christ. It is this which we have to put into the empty frame of the new social order. It is this which no social order can give but which those men who strove for it in the name of Christ had in mind. It is this which the new social order is craving for.

The Gospel of Jesus Christ is the same in all ages. But the task of the Church, given by His Gospel and constituted by it, is not the same but different in every epoch. Every age has to rediscover Christ anew—no Christ dogma can give what this rediscovery is intended to give. The Christ dogma is a mere intellectual substitute for the continuity of the living Church through the living Lord. Still we can see that what the great Christians were after in previous ages is the same as we are after in our day. They all tried to interpret the Gospel of the saving grace and truth in such a way that by it men's lives are transformed from those of self-centred, lonely individualists into members of the Body of Christ.

During the last generation we had a social Gospel, following the generation of the great revivals of individual conversion. What we need now is a new social Gospel, but different from that of the last generation in that it does not strive for a social *order* but for personal community. We also need a new revival, but not one which is concerned merely with the saving of souls but which, again, seeks the true personal life in a real communion with God and man. We need a personalistic communism and a sacramental existentialism, which would fill the empty frame of the new social order, and at the same time fulfil the highest aspirations of those who created it. But let us be reassured that it is neither the Church nor the social order which ultimately matter, but the *Ekklesia*, the Body of Christ into which no one enters but through the Word and grace of God.